A Co

Leon-Joseph Cardinal Suenens

A Controversial Phenomenon
Resting in the Spirit

VERITAS PUBLICATIONS

First published 1987 by
Veritas Publications
7-8 Lower Abbey Street
Dublin 1

Copyright © 1987 Leon-Joseph Cardinal Suenens

ISBN 0 86217 208 X

Extracts from the *Revised Standard Version* of the Bible, copyright 1946, 1952, 1971 by the Division of Christian Education of the National Council of the Churches of Christ in the USA; reproduced with permission. If any involuntary infringement of copyright has occurred, sincere apologies are offered and the owner of such copyright is requested to contact the publisher.

Cover design: David Cooke
Typesetting: Printset & Design Ltd
Printed in the Republic of Ireland by
Mount Salus Press Ltd

Contents

Preface   7

PART ONE: DESCRIPTIVE

1. The issue of the debate   11
2. 'Resting in the Spirit'?   17
3. Antecedents and analogies   25
4. 'Resting in the Spirit' as a mass phenomenon   29

PART TWO: CRITICAL

5. Are there references in the Bible?   37
6. Are there references in the mystical writers?   41
7. The ambiguity of bodily manifestations in general   47
8. The sovereign freedom and discretion of the Holy Spirit   51

PART THREE: PASTORAL

9. Are the 'fruits' a decisive criterion?   57
10. Dangers inherent in the experience   61
11. Is it a natural phenomenon or a sign of the Holy Spirit's action?   67
12. On the necessity of caution   73
      Conclusion   79

Preface

This sixth *Malines Document* is devoted to the study of a phenomenon known as 'resting in the Spirit', which is provoking controversies and very divergent reactions. How are we to interpret this phenomenon?

'Resting in the Spirit' is a divisive issue. Because it has become a widespread practice, both within the Renewal and outside its sphere of influence, I requested the International Charismatic Catholic Renewal Office (ICCRO), established in Rome, to act as my intermediary and to invite people with some experience of the phenomenon and a considered opinion (whether positive or negative) on the subject, to send me their testimony as a contribution to the present study.

I received a great many replies: their analysis considerably slowed down the publication of this study. These many reactions came from every continent, but especially from Europe. Usually, the answers were personal, but some were collective, having been compiled from the questionnaires of local surveys.

Since it is impossible to thank each of my kind correspondents personally, I take this opportunity to express my deep gratitude to them and to the ICCRO for their valuable cooperation.

My initial intention had been to devote this sixth *Malines Document* to the positive promotion of the ministry and charism of healing. But in the light of this new issue, it was desirable to begin by clearing the ground and attempting to discern whether or not we are beholding a new intervention of the Spirit, a new mode of healing, an unprecedented grace given to our time.

Part One of this *Malines Document* is devoted to a description of the phenomenon *per se,* in an historical, biblical and mystical perspective. Part Two is a critical examination of the phenomenon. And Part Three attempts to discern and specify the prudential pastoral attitude which I believe to be essential in our approach to 'Resting in the Spirit'.

L.-J. Cardinal SUENENS
January 1986

PART ONE: Descriptive

1

THE ISSUE OF THE DEBATE

This sixth *Malines Document* is devoted to the discernment of an ambiguous and controversial phenomenon which has received various names, such as 'resting in the Spirit' and 'slain in the Spirit'. I shall return to this point presently.

But before examining the phenomenon as such, I would like to explain briefly what the 'Charismatic Movement' itself is, so that we may be in a better position to locate the precise topic of this study and to identify the issues of the wider debate.

THE RENEWAL: AN 'OPPORTUNITY TO BE SEIZED'

I. What the Renewal is not
Paradoxically, the best way of introducing and defining the Renewal is to explain what the 'Charismatic Movement' is not.

For as long as we envisage the Charismatic Renewal as just one of several spiritual 'movements', we are losing sight of its specific grace which is permeating the Church.

In fact, it is not a movement in the usual sociological sense of the term: it has no founders and no leaders, institutionalised or even recognised as such by the Church. It does not form a homogeneous whole, but has numerous variants, and it imposes no precise obligations on its members.

It can best be described as a 'current of grace', an 'actual grace' (to use the theological term), a movement or breath of the Holy Spirit, valid for every Christian, regardless of the 'movement' to which he belongs, regardless of whether he is a lay person, a religious, a priest or a bishop. We are on the wrong track from the start if we raise the question of departments and ask: can you be, at one and the same time, a member of a particular body or community and a member of the Renewal? The answer can only be the old scholastic formula *nego suppositum* (the premise is false).

We do not 'enter' the Renewal: it is the Renewal which enters into us, if we accept its grace. One cannot be both a Franciscan and a Jesuit, but it is perfectly possible to be a Franciscan open to the Renewal, or a 'charismatic' Jesuit, without having to leave one's order.

Moreover, the adjective 'charismatic', applied to the Renewal, is not an apt term: it is ambiguous in more than one respect.

First, because the word itself has no exclusive significance: the whole Church is charismatic; each and every Christian is charismatic by virtue of his baptism and confirmation, whether or not he is aware of it.

The term 'charismatic' unnecessarily offends outside observers, and it is sometimes misunderstood even in groups who quote it as their authority. In these circumstances, people all too easily regard the charisms as gifts which they possess: gifts received from God, undoubtedly, but of which they are the sole agents. Kevin Ranaghan, one of the pioneers of the Renewal in the United States, recently protested against this 'reifying' interpretation.

When one lays emphasis on the charisms, however real they may be, one easily forgets that the first gift of the Spirit is the Spirit himself, that the grace *par excellence* is the God-centred grace of growth in faith, hope and love, and that love is the supreme test of Christian authenticity.

Lastly, people readily focus all their attention on the so-called extraordinary charisms — the only ones that enthrall the mass media — and fail to appreciate the 'ordinary' charisms which are the Church's daily bread and nourish the Christian life.

It is interesting to read a speech of John Paul II to the bishops of Belgium in which, without once using the term, he enumerates a series of *ordinary charisms* that are essential to the Church's

Descriptive

vitality.[1] At the Vatican Council, I urged, from the same viewpoint, that the ordinary charisms of the faithful be fully recognised in the life of the Church.[2]

When we over-emphasise the role and place of the extraordinary charisms and see them as 'one-off' and therefore transitory gifts, we are liable to overlook the permanent charisms inherent in the 'institutional' Church. I am thinking here of the Spirit's Anointing, which rests on bishops, priests and deacons and is inherent in the Church's sacramental structure.

We know that in Scripture the term 'charism' has various meanings. The original Greek word means 'gift', and the gifts of God are many and varied. In the language of Scripture, St Paul uses the word very freely. So we ought to handle it prudently.

Well, what term should we use? If we wish to convey as accurately as possible the reality underlying our vocabulary, I believe that the most adequate term would be *Pentecostal Renewal*. It instantly draws attention to the essential nature of the Renewal: namely, that it is a spiritual renewal arising from and perpetuating the specific grace of Pentecost.

The first disciples lived the original Pentecost, which is constitutive of the Church as:
—the grace of conversion,
—the grace of discovering the living Christ,
—the grace of welcoming the Spirit, his power and his gifts.

'Pentecostal Renewal' translates the full breadth of the Holy Spirit's action: he embraces and vivifies every aspect of the Church. This tremendous fact urges us to welcome the Spirit's dynamic purpose. 'I shall send you my Spirit . . . and you will be my witnesses. . . .'

It urges us to perpetuate the Acts of the Apostles in today's history. As we know, John XXIII asked the bishops to prepare for the Council by rereading the Acts.

Vatican II was a Pentecostal grace for all the bishops,

---

1. *Dec. Catholique,* 17 October 1982, p. 910.
2. L.-J. Suenens, *Coresponsibility in the Church,* London, Burns & Oates, 1968.

throughout the world. For my part, I believe that the Pentecostal Renewal is a spiritual continuation of the Council, and that it is offered to each Christian as a grace of spiritual revitalisation, in the line of Pentecost. It was certainly in this light that Paul VI understood it when he welcomed some 10,000 'charismatic' pilgrims to St Peter's in Rome. His speech on that occasion remains the charter, as it were, of the Renewal, which he called 'an opportunity for the Church'.

II. An opportunity entailing risks

An opportunity to be seized, a precious grace which we should not miss by failing to recognise the signs of God.

An opportunity to be seized: this implies that wherever the Holy Spirit is at work, the Spirit of evil is on the watch, ready to distort, to destabilise and to destroy.

At the Council, during a tense moment, my friend Helder Camara said to me: 'If the devil weren't prowling around just now, he'd be an idiot!' The same is true of the circumstances surrounding the Renewal. We should not be surprised to find the devil creating a number of counterfeits of the authentic Renewal or trying to introduce deviations into a work of God. In the final reckoning, it is incumbent on the discernment of the bishops, mandated by the Lord, to distinguish the true from the false and to recognise the signs of God in the weakness and obtuseness of men.

Therefore 'an opportunity to be seized' also means one not to be lost through the introduction of non-authenticated charisms.

And this danger leads us directly to the examination of the marginal phenomenon known as 'resting in the Spirit' — a phenomenon more widespread than it is thought to be.

Very often, the local bishop does not even know that it is being practised in his diocese, because its practitioners avoid telling him about it and submitting it to his discernment, or because only a muffled echo of it reaches the ears of the religious authorities.

We all know how fascinated and intrigued the public is by extraordinary happenings, such as visions, apparitions, miraculous healings, and so forth.

Descriptive

So we have to be most careful not to threaten the very credibility of the Renewal.

In fact, in the current debate which sets in opposition two interpretations of the same phenomenon, we are dealing with two ways of envisaging the relations between nature and grace; but it is important not to bypass the secondary causes. Further on I shall return to this point. But first I would like to describe the phenomenon itself in greater detail, with the help of direct testimonies.

2

'RESTING IN THE SPIRIT'?

What does 'resting in the Spirit' mean? I shall begin by describing the phenomenon as perceived by those who have experienced it.

I. Description

Generally speaking, the term designates a phenomenon of falling (usually backwards), and it is quite frequently connected with a healing or prayer service. Observed objectively, this visible bodily action can be described by a whole range of verbs: falling, sliding to the ground, collapsing, sinking down, letting go, lying down, swaying, becoming rigid, and so on.

The habitual terms, inherited from Pentecostalism and habitually used in various charismatic circles, are:
— 'Slain in the Spirit'; or
— 'Overpowering of the Spirit'; or
— 'Resting in the Spirit'; or
— 'The Blessing'.

From the viewpoint of the insider, all these terms imply that the phenomenon is linked with a particular action of the Holy Spirit. Since it is precisely this interpretation which is problematic and controversial, the first question that arises — even before we embark on a critical analysis and opt for a pastoral attitude — is to reach agreement about the vocabulary itself.

II. Vocabulary

An Anglican minister, J. Richards, suggests that, to begin with, we should adopt a neutral term that remains purely descriptive and does not make its spiritual content and interpretation a foregone conclusion. He proposes that we call it 'the falling phenomenon', and not speak too hastily of 'resting in the Spirit', for the debatable point, in this context, is precisely the role of the Spirit. Falling, as such, is a visible, natural phenomenon; whereas falling as a result of the Holy Spirit's action would — if such an interpretation were correct — be of the supernatural order.

And since the natural level must be distinguished from the supernatural, a 'neutral' vocabulary leaves the way open for serene study and discussion. I note that two other writers, respectively American and German, concur with J. Richards, and I too endorse his suggestion. In short, I shall more frequently speak of 'falling' than of 'resting'.

In varying degrees, the phenomenon is found among Christians of the mainstream Churches — whether Catholic, Anglican or Lutheran — and more particularly among those who, in former days, were awakened by 'revivals', or in our time by Pentecostalism, which sprang up at the beginning of this century. But it was especially after World War II that the phenomenon began to occur in the main Christian denominations, and more recently in the Catholic Church.

It is not easy to describe the 'falling' phenomenon in an absolute way, for it has numerous variants. But I shall try to elicit a kind of common denominator.

III. Listening to testimonies

As I said earlier, I received, in response to my appeal through the ICCRO, a great many testimonies from all over the world. They attest to the universality of the phenomenon and deserve to be studied attentively.

In order to avoid needless repetitions, I am grouping the answers I received under the main questions put to the respondents.

At this stage, I am abstaining from critical reflections in order to let the witnesses speak of their own experiences, and also of their deductions and interpretations.

1. What kind of people fall?
2. How is the phenomenon triggered off?
3. In what context does it occur?

4. What do people feel when they are about to fall?
5. Can they resist the impulse?
6. What do they feel when they fall?
7. What help should be offered at this time?
8. What do they feel after falling?
9. What are the alleged fruits of this experience?

1. What kind of people fall?

I note first of all that a wide variety of people fall; but most frequently cited are:
— Women (in the majority);
— people suffering from depression and other psychic problems;
— people harbouring strong resentment towards others;
— people trying to cope with difficult personal situations, such as married couples in a state of tension and conflict;
— people who are not in the least expecting to fall and do not even know what is happening to them;
— sometimes, but more rarely, children;
— subjects in need of spiritual and emotional healing, rather than those suffering from a physical illness.

2. How is the falling triggered off?

This question springs naturally to mind.
Here are a few of the answers I received:
— by well-known personalities who are, so to speak, specialists in the field and attract large audiences;
— by persons who habitually pray for others and, with no previous experience of the phenomenon, suddenly and unexpectedly find people falling at their touch;
— at one and the same meeting, subjects may fall under the action of one person, but not of another;
— various witnesses state that they do not know what causes others to fall when they pray over them; they are simply aware that it happens, but can offer no explanation.

3. In what context does 'falling' occur?

Judging by the answers, the context is very varied:
— sometimes the phenomenon occurs in a vast assembly of

several thousand people, and therefore in an atmosphere conducive to suggestion on the part of lay healers or specialised priests;
— it can also happen in a small prayer group where no one has fallen previously;
— more often than not, it occurs at meetings where the participants are expecting it and a small team is ready to take care of the falling subjects. In particular, it occurs during a healing service;
— at times the phenomenon is triggered off in groups after a 'professional' has visited them; there are also cases where it ceases after a while, although the group leaders do not really know why;
— there are also known cases where it occurs without prayer, laying on of hands or similar gestures;
— not infrequently, it occurs in the context of a eucharistic celebration.

4. What do people feel when they are about to fall?

A variety of experiences may occur:
— a sensation of being pushed over by an invisible force, a pressure being felt on the person's forehead, chest or thighs;
— a feeling of gradually becoming weaker until, unable to resist any longer, the subject falls to the ground;
— some find themselves on the floor without knowing how it occurred;
— often there is a feeling of relaxation and weightlessness;
— some have a sensation of their feet being lifted off the ground before they fall;
— although some people fall heavily, they are in such a relaxed state that they rarely injure themselves;
— generally, people fall backwards;
— the persons praying over the subject usually lay their hands on his head, and sometimes give his forehead a gentle push or anoint it with oil;
— falling can also occur without physical contact with or proximity to the subject;

Descriptive

— sometimes the phenomenon occurs when no witnesses are present;
— some people tremble and sway but do not fall, although they have the same sensations as those who drop to the floor;
— some state that when they are falling, they feel loss of control rather than loss of consciousness.

5. Can they resist?

Most of my correspondents tell me that people can resist the impulse if they wish to. Nevertheless they sometimes fall in spite of their scepticism, resistance or guardedness.

But they are advised to offer no resistance, so as (I quote) 'to enable God to act when the subject is on the floor in a relaxed position'.

6. What do they experience when they fall?

This question is of special interest, for the answers are many and varied.

Here are a few of the reported sensations; they are not classified and follow no particular order:
— a sense of a special presence of God, a feeling of euphoria and peace;
— 'we remain conscious, but our eyes are closed and we hear sounds around us, although in some cases the sounds seem to be far away';
— some may be unconscious or have only a vague recollection of events afterwards;
— most feel that they could get up, but have no desire to do so. However, some feel that they are unable to get up;
— a few have sensory experiences, such as being aware of a sweet smelling fragrance or hearing sounds like a choir singing;
— some have mental images or 'visions' which put them 'in contact with God and the supernatural world';
— others hear 'voices' and have a sense of God 'conveying messages' to comfort or guide them;
— in some cases, the subject bursts into tears, cries out or laughs uncontrollably.

7. What help should be offered at this time?

This question concerns the pastoral care to be offered when the phenomenon occurs. In reading the following answers, the reader will note the detailed precautions taken.

— Helpers, known as 'catchers', should stand behind those about to fall backwards, in order to break their fall and prevent them from collapsing on top of those already lying on the ground.
— If no catchers are available, the healer should place his hand on the subject's back or support his neck, so that he may not fall too heavily when 'slain in the Spirit'.
— If someone falls unexpectedly 'under the power of the Spirit', the helpers must be ready to lay him out comfortably and to straighten his legs if they have buckled under him.
— There is no further need to pray for those who have already fallen and are 'resting in the Spirit', for 'the Lord is already at work in them'.
— Some respondents even specify that the helpers should have a blanket at hand to cover the legs of women who have fallen awkwardly and thus save them embarrassment.

In connection with our present investigation, I note that some advocates of the 'falling phenomenon' believe that objections could be overcome if the subjects were seated, for in this way all the disadvantages of falling backwards could be avoided.

A curious detail: I read in a booklet of official guidelines recently issued by the Hartford diocese (USA) that many people who desire to be 'touched by the Spirit' are unwilling to adopt the sitting position, since they feel that it would thwart the action of the Holy Spirit. To this objection, the booklet replies, with good sense, that the Holy Spirit does not allow himself to be hindered by such considerations.

8. What do people experience after falling?

Here are some of the answers that reached me:
— most people state that they feel spiritually, emotionally and physically refreshed. They have a sense of lightness, peace and joy which may last for several hours or days and is often accompanied by the desire to praise God.

— if they stand up too soon, before returning to 'normal', they may feel weak and faint, and may need to sit or lie down until full strength returns.
— some experience fear and confusion. This, it is believed, usually occurs when 'God' brings to the surface fears, tensions or resentments buried in the subconscious; and it is a sign, we are told, that the person may need counselling and more prayers for healing.

9. What are the 'fruits'?

The fruits most frequently cited by my correspondents are:
— the alleviation of psychic disturbances;
— almost total healing of profound psychic problems;
— the healing of inner wounds and resentments;
— the healing of damaged relationships (marriage, etc.);
— feelings of peace;
— new possibilities of forgiving, or repenting;
— a love of prayer and Scripture; a depth of encounter with Jesus;
— some physical healings (rare).

3

ANTECEDENTS AND ANALOGIES

I. In Christian circles

The phenomenon we are examining was by no means unknown or unusual in the past. The Church has regularly to come to grips with more or less analogous bodily manifestations.

Father George A. Maloney, SJ, founder of the John XXIII Institute for the Study of Eastern Spiritualities, attached to Fordham University (USA), tells us in a study devoted to 'resting in the Spirit' that this phenomenon — known among the traditional Pentecostals as 'slain in the Spirit' — is regarded by many Catholic Charismatics as something quite new in our time. But he points out that, in fact, it is an ancient phenomenon, commonly found in the history of groups called 'Enthusiasts', and especially in the revivals of New England and the West in the seventeenth and nineteenth centuries.

Here I shall confine myself to a brief survey.

Monsignor Ronald Knox wrote the classic work on the subject: *Enthusiasm* (Oxford Ed., 1973). The subtitle tells us that his study is devoted mainly to the history of these manifestations in the seventeenth and eighteenth centuries.

This book has been, as it were, updated by James Hitchcock, Professor of History in the University of St Louis (USA), under the provocative title *The New Enthusiasts and What They Are Doing to the Catholic Church* (Chicago, Thomas More Press, 1982).

As an illustration, here are a few lines from the *Journal* of John Wesley, the founder of Methodism. He relates the experience undergone by his circle on 1 January 1739 after a prayer service:

About three in the morning, as we were continuing instant

in prayer, the power of God came mightily upon us, insomuch that many cried out for exceeding joy, and many fell to the ground.

At first, John Wesley rejoiced in the phenomenon, taking it to be a sign from God: but a later entry in his *Journal* (4 June 1772) informs us that these manifestations, though frequent in the early days, subsequently became exceptional.

The same type of phenomenon also occurred at the first meetings of the Salvation Army (founded by William Booth in 1878), and was called 'having a holy fit'.

At the time of the great religious revival of the late eighteenth century, a variety of sects — including one known as 'the Shakers' — experienced the phenomenon on a large scale, with dramatic effects, such as loss of consciousness, convulsions, and so on.

Nearer to our time, the evangelist George Jeffreys, founder of the Elim Foursquare Gospel Alliance (1915) — which gave a strong impulse to the Pentecostal movement between 1925 and 1953 — underlined and studied the phenomenon. He recognised the excesses of the physical manifestations accompanying the great revivals of 1859 and 1904, but he attributed these to the resistance offered to the Spirit by some who, as he put it, inevitably became the victims of their denial.

Doubtless today's 'falling phenomenon' usually occurs without the excesses of 'trances' and 'ecstasies', but we still need to know whether or not these three states are related.

II. Outside Christianity

Looking beyond the Christian world, we find bodily manifestations which are, to some extent, analogous.

These are encountered in certain religious experiences that are a prelude to a new state of soul, and they are perceived as a mysterious contact with the divinity, usually engendering a feeling of peace and 'transference' to another world. At times falling to the ground and a partial loss of consciousness accompany these experiences.

'Trance', 'ecstasy' and 'rapture' are also well-known in this context. Etymologically, the very word 'trance' is expressive of a 'transition' from one state of being to another. And 'ecstasy' denotes that the spirit is, as it were, carried out of the body, out of time and space. As we know, the disciples of the Buddha and Mahomet stress the role played by trance and ecstasy in the spiritual awakening of these founders.

Moreover, it is important to bear in mind that the phenomenon also occurs in some Eastern sects. Mircea Eliade has made a detailed and exemplary study of this subject in his book, *Shamanism*.[1]

And the study of 'trances' among primitive African and Latin American tribes gives scientific research in this area an even wider field of investigation.

Lastly, no detailed study can overlook 'analogies' encountered in a wholly secular context. One is reminded of the amazing physical reactions (including fainting fits) of large audiences at jazz festivals and pop concerts.

None of these experiences entitles us to make too hasty a judgment about the phenomenon we are witnessing today; but it is both necessary and useful to consider manifestations which bear some analogy to it, if only because they bring home to us that this is a delicate area of investigation which calls for extra discernment on the part of Christians desiring to remain faithful to the Church's authentic tradition.

---

1. *Shamanism, Archaic Technique of Ecstasy,* New Jersey, Princeton University Press, 1964.

4

'RESTING IN THE SPIRIT' AS A MASS PHENOMENON

I. Kathryn Kuhlman

Quite recently the phenomenon suddenly awakened fresh interest in the United States as a result of the ministry of healing exercised by a striking personality, the Baptist healer Kathryn Kuhlman (d. 1976).

She comes into this study because of the spectacular nature of her healing services, in which the 'falling phenomenon' played a prominent role. The media made her famous in the United States, Canada and other countries. Thousands of people would regularly flock to her services. Her ministry of healing was accompanied by a powerful buildup of music and singing, and skilful 'catchers' would gently ease to the floor those on whom she placed her hands.

Various studies have been devoted to Kathryn Kuhlman, either to extol her ministry or to cast doubt on her personality and her healings. My purpose here is not to take sides on this issue, since at this stage I am still describing the phenomenon as such.

Among the many descriptions I have read or heard from witnesses, I have selected an account sent to me by an American priest, for I consider it both typical and thought-provoking. Moreover, my correspondent's testimony is of special interest because he was himself a member of a team of priests exercising a healing ministry, which usually involved the 'falling phenomenon', though in a less sensational manner. This is what he writes:

> I first came in contact with 'slaying in the Spirit' in 1972 when I attended a Kathryn Kuhlman healing service in

New York City. The service was held in a large ballroom of the Americana Hotel. Some thousands of people filled the ballroom and overflowed into other rooms with the sound piped to them. There was an obvious expectant faith in many of those present. This expectancy pervaded the whole ballroom. There were introductory speakers and much singing — a buildup for the dramatic entrance of Kathryn Kuhlman.

She entered, walking up the aisle in a long, flowing gown, and smiling. She led all in prayer and encouraged more singing. This was followed by a twenty to thirty minute sermon which, though not profoundly oratorical, was sincere and faith-stirring. To me, she was a woman who loved Jesus Christ and preached Him. Time after time during the service she verbally gave all the glory to God for the success of her work. After speaking for about twenty to thirty minutes, she paused, as if listening, and then announced that someone was being healed of a certain ailment — even describing the general location of that person in the ballroom.

The healing service was well organised in that many ushers attended the aisles and some of these ushers escorted to the stage people who 'claimed' or thought they had been healed. When they arrived at the stage, Kathryn Kuhlman would question them about their illness and healing. This was in full view of stage lights. As the healing was announced, the audience responded by applause or loud verbal thanks to God.

My correspondent relates that one of his parishioners, who had come with him, stated that he had been healed of cancer, which provoked much enthusiasm. Then he was himself invited to come to the stage by Kathryn Kuhlman, who laid her hands on his forehead. He writes that he then felt a definite physical 'pushing' of his head backwards and was tempted to resist it, but finally allowed himself to fall backwards, too, into the arms of an usher. He immediately got to his feet, fully conscious, and without feeling that the experience had affected him in any way.

The service lasted about three to four hours.

Later, my correspondent renewed the experience by attending another healing service held by Kathryn Kuhlman in a Presbyterian church in Pittsburgh, Pennsylvania. At a vigil prior to the service, some members of Kathryn Kuhlman's entourage told him that he too had the power to 'slay in the Spirit'. They asked him to lay hands on them, which he did, and they fell backwards to the floor.

Subsequently, he practised this newly-discovered method of healing occasionally, for a few years, at priests' retreats, but not otherwise. However, as time went on, and in the light of experience, he came to understand its dangers and finally abandoned it.

The testimony he sent me ends with the following reflections, which I am summarising:
— today, he feels that the power in question is a natural psychic force which might sometimes, and exceptionally, be used by grace but ought not to be ranked among the supernatural charisms.
— a real danger, in his view, is that it may damage the Catholic Charismatic Renewal and cause it to deviate from its real purpose.
— he notes, in passing, that the parishioner who accompanied him and announced that he was healed of cancer, died a few months later.
— he ends with a heartfelt appeal to bishops and leaders in the Renewal to break their silence and give adequate guidance on the subject of 'resting in the Spirit'.

II. Present spread of the phenomenon in Catholic circles
1. The ecumenical climate

The spread of the phenomenon in Catholic circles can be explained, in part, by the postconciliar climate of ecumenical openness, which is sometimes translated into a facile ecumenism, tending to unite Christians — and not the Christian Churches — on the basis of the smallest common denominator, and in direct reference to the Holy Spirit. A one-sided emphasis on the role of the Holy Spirit, to the detriment of natural, human mediations, has undoubtedly fostered the warm response to this special kind of 'charism'.

Moreover, encounters between Catholics and the Pentecostal and Free Churches have also had an influence on the present practice of 'resting in the Spirit'.

It is well-known that, in the early days of the Charismatic Renewal, some non-Catholic leaders were astonished to see the Church of Rome welcoming the Renewal in the Spirit. Equally memorable and surprising was the sensational message addressed to Catholics by David Wilkerson, the author of the famous book *The Cross and the Dagger:* 'Either you leave the Church or the Holy Spirit will leave you!' To which the Catholics replied vigorously, through the pen of Ralph Martin, affirming their twofold fidelity to the Holy Spirit and the Church. But that was no more than a skirmish.

As to the specific point that concerns us here, how can we ever forget the well-founded warning issued by David du Plessis (the representative of the Pentecostal Churches at Vatican Council II) when he beseeched Catholics to avoid the mistake made by Pentecostals in the past, and not to introduce the 'falling phenomenon', which had given them nothing but trouble.

2. Internationalisation

To all these factors of diffusion and interpretation we must naturally add the increasingly accentuated internationalisation of today's world.

The 'resting' phenomenon has not remained confined to its birthplaces, where at the moment it appears to be slowing down. Over the last few years it has rapidly spread worldwide, and this is due, in part, to the present internationalisation of our planet.

Missionaries who had encountered the phenomenon, mainly in the United States, made themselves the propagandists of what they regarded as a charism for our time, given by the Lord to his Church. Imitators of Kathryn Kuhlman sprouted up like mushrooms, attracting the crowds in their own turn and becoming centres of attraction.

Here I shall cite merely a few names, without analysing the

persons concerned or their work. The most influential propagandist during the seventies was the ex-Dominican priest Francis MacNutt (USA), whose style was reminiscent of Kathryn Kuhlman's and whose popular works were widely read in Catholic circles and accepted by some very literally and uncritically.

A few years ago, I personally took part in a seminar for psychiatrists and moralists, held by Francis MacNutt in Florida. On that occasion, I attended 'slain in the Spirit' sessions where people would line up before him to receive laying on of hands, then fall to the ground one after the other.

Other popularisers have achieved renown in this field; they include Father de Grandis, SJ, and Father di Orio who wrote his autobiography as a 'Master of Healing' under the somewhat curious title *A Man Behind the Gift*. In Europe, some retreat masters have also decided to specialise in the same line.

The mass media have played an important part in the popularisation of this phenomenon, which feeds the public's taste for the sensational.

All this creates a real problem.

In conclusion, I think I am right in saying that the 'falling phenomenon' is giving rise to unease and leaves a number of question marks, both in Catholic circles and in other Christian Churches.

How should we interpret it? I repeat my initial question: are we dealing with a special intervention of the Holy Spirit, 'a charism for our time', or with a natural phenomenon which — in some cases and under certain circumstances — can be beneficial?

In Part Two I shall attempt to come to grips with this question and to help the Renewal in its task of discernment.

But before we move on to the direct, critical study of 'resting in the Spirit', it would be appropriate to ask ourselves whether the advocates of the phenomenon who quote the Bible and the mystical writers in support of their claims are interpreting their sources correctly. So the following chapter will examine the biblical and mystical references which they adduce in favour of the supernatural interpretation.

PART TWO: Critical

5

ARE THERE REFERENCES IN THE BIBLE?

To avoid all confusion, we must keep well in mind the description of the phenomenon we are studying before we start looking for corroborative references in Scripture.

The passages of Scripture which deal with 'falling down' or being 'thrown to the ground' by the power of God's majesty, or simply with 'sleeping', correspond neither to phenomena of the Kathryn Kuhlman type, nor to the 'resting' which some of our witnesses have presented in gentler terms as 'a peaceful and conscious physical surrender to God's healing work'.

Anyone rereading the description of the falling phenomenon provided earlier in chapter 2 will realise that Scripture's accounts of falling to the ground in the presence of God's majesty describe another order of experience.

There is no record in those scriptural passages of a person receiving imposition of hands from another person, or from a group in prayer, and there is no mention of falling **backwards**. Usually, Scripture speaks of people falling **forward** in worship, with their foreheads touching the ground.

When the Bible describes people 'falling to the ground before God', it is not always easy to distinguish whether this response is a conscious and willed act of worship, or an act of surrender to the power of God, or simply a manifestation of obedience. Numerous examples of falling are recorded in the Old and New Testaments, and in the Acts of the Apostles, but they have none of the distinctive traits of the 'falling phenomenon' and are of a very different nature.

Here it will suffice to read a few of the adduced passages to realise that they are not analogous to or identical with the phenomenon we are examining.

A Controversial Phenomenon

As examples, and without attempting to give an exhaustive list, I indicate below the main passages often quoted in support of the supernaturalist interpretation of the phenomenon.

I. In the Old Testament
Ezekiel 1:28:
   I saw what looked like the glory of the Lord. When I saw it, I fell upon my face, and I heard a voice speaking.

Daniel 10:7-9:
   I, Daniel, alone saw the vision . . . and when I heard the sound of his words, I fell unconscious with my face on the ground.

Genesis 15:12:
   As the sun was setting, a deep sleep fell on Abram; and a dread and great darkness fell upon him.

Joshua 5:14:
   'No', he replied, 'I am commander of the army of the Lord, and I have now come.' Joshua fell on his face to the ground and said to him, 'What does my lord bid his servant?'

II. In the New Testament
Some claim to find analogies in:
— Matthew 17:6: The disciples fall on their face, overcome by the Transfiguration.
— John 18:6: The soldiers arresting Jesus move back and fall to the ground.
— Acts 9:4: The conversion of Saul, who falls to the ground on the road to Damascus.
— Matthew 28:1-4: On Easter morning the guards 'trembled and became like dead men'.
— Revelation 1:17: St John describes his vision and ends with the words: 'When I saw him, I fell in a dead faint at his feet. He touched me with his right hand and said, "Do not be afraid".'

   One has only to read these texts to see how much they differ from the 'falling phenomenon'.

— The soldiers who draw back on beholding the majesty of Jesus are in no sense experiencing a mystical grace of 'resting in the Spirit'. They are momentarily overcome by his majesty, but then go on to arrest him.
— Saul does fall to the ground on the road to Damascus. But his fall, due to the dazzling light of the Risen Christ, cannot be likened to a 'spiritual anaesthesia': it is a radical conversion, a discovery, followed by the Lord's instruction to go and find Ananias, in order to learn what God requires of the new apostle whom he has called to his service.
— The disciples who fall to the ground on Mount Tabor immediately react, through their spokesman Peter, with a stammering request to their Master: 'Let us make three tents: one for you, one for Moses, and one for Elijah.' None of this corresponds to the manifestations described as 'resting in the Spirit'.

In conclusion

The comparative study of scriptural texts and the 'falling phenomenon' has not yet, to my knowledge, been the subject of exegetical researches focusing on our topic. So here I confine myself to three testimonies which I would like to communicate to my readers; and these clearly point out the disparity between the scriptural events and the 'falling phenomenon'.

Father George Maloney, SJ, having examined some of the biblical references, concludes:

> In all of these we do not find the same phenomenon known as 'slaying in the Spirit'. Ecstasy is not the same as one falling into a faint through the mediation of another than Jesus Christ. I fail to find a parallel for this phenomenon. We know that power went out of Peter and Paul and all the Disciples as they preached and healed. It is quite evident from the Acts. But there does not seem to be a basis for believing people swooned in a faint when they prayed over the fullness of the Holy Spirit.

His view tallies with that of John Richards, an Anglican minister who has specialised in the subject and who, in his study entitled 'Resting in the Spirit', published in the review *Renewal in Wales Today* (No. 6, Spring 1984), reaches a similar conclusion.

A third writer who comes to the same conclusion is the Lutheran theologian and pastor Wolfram Kopfermann, in his article in the German review *Rundbrief der charismatischen Gemeinde — Erneuerung in der evangelischen Kirche* (June 1983, pp. 19-25).

I too am of the opinion that there is no biblical foundation for the swooning brought about by the touch of a healer, in the manner of Kathryn Kuhlman. It is important to realise that falling to the ground does not always have the same significance, and that there is an essential difference between falling forward and falling backward. Falling forward is a profound, natural response which can be motivated by a feeling of respect and humility. Falling backward, on the other hand, is hardly natural and suggests that the subject is, as it were, seized by some alien force. I should add that even falling on one's face, or prostration, receives little scriptural encouragement, for in the examples quoted earlier there are three cases *(Dn 10:11; Ez 2:1; Mt 17:6-7)* where God bids the affected persons to stand up.

6

ARE THERE REFERENCES IN THE MYSTICAL WRITERS?

I. The Church's prudence

As I said earlier, the Church has frequently been faced, in the course of history, with phenomena of interaction between body, soul and mind. The more a psychic reaction has repercussions on the body, the more discernment becomes essential. In the canonisation process, the Church is careful to distinguish the attributes of authentic sanctity (which is founded on the theological virtues of faith, hope and love) from what pertains to exterior bodily manifestations, such as ecstasy, levitation, the stigmata, and so on.

Pius XII gave a typical example of this prudence in 1940 on the occasion of the canonisation of Sister Gemma Galgani. He was careful to state that he authenticated her sanctity not by reason of certain bodily phenomena evidenced in her life, but despite these, for he did not hesitate to associate them with certain neurotic tendencies. There could be no clearer way of saying that the two aspects are distinct.

Yet another sign of the Church's prudence lies in the insistence with which it has always made a distinction between the charisms that sanctify the recipient, making him pleasing to God (which is the meaning of the classical Latin expression *gratum faciens*) and the charisms whose direct object is the good of the community, its edification in the constructive sense of 'upbuilding the whole community'; the latter gifts do not necessarily sanctify their recipient and instrument. They are given gratuitously *(gratis datae)* for a use that transcends the person and with a view to serving the community in a particular way.

II. A confusion to be avoided

To substantiate the supernatural interpretation of the falling phenomenon, some of its proponents adduce mystical 'analogies' which, in their view, belong to the same family of phenomena. Accordingly, they compare 'resting in the Spirit' with the repose of the soul or even the prayer of quiet. But it must be clearly stated that we are dealing with two wholly different levels of experience.

1. Resting in the Spirit and the repose of the soul

This is what St Francis de Sales writes about the repose of the soul:

> The soul being thus recollected in God or before God sometimes becomes so gently attentive to the goodness of its Beloved that its attention, it feels, can hardly be called that, so simply and delicately does it exercise this function, in the likeness of some rivers which flow so gently and evenly that those watching them or sailing on them would say they can see or feel no movement at all because their ripples and undulations are imperceptible. It is this sweet repose of the soul that the blessed virgin Teresa of Jesus calls the prayer of quiet, which hardly differs from what she herself refers to as the sleep of the faculties, if I have understood her correctly *(Treatise on the Love of God, Book VI, ch. 8)*.

If we now compare this resting of the soul with 'resting in the Spirit', we immediately realise that they are wholly different spiritual experiences, their only common feature being the word 'resting', which, in the second case, is used most ambiguously.

2. Resting in the Spirit and the prayer of quiet

'Resting in the Spirit' has also been described as a form of the prayer of quiet. Questioned by me on this point, the Irish Carmelite theologian Father Christopher O'Donnell, a professor of mystical theology, replied as follows:

The prayer of quiet is very diverse in forms. It can be dark and it can be light. The descriptions of it are very deceptive: it is easy to confuse prayer of recollection (more or less the Third Mansion) with prayer of quiet, especially for those who do not have great experience of prayer of quiet.

I suppose my problem in brief might be expressed thus: what is accomplished by saying that 'slaying in the Spirit', when genuine, resembles the prayer of quiet? There are no shortcuts to high sanctity, and the habitual reception of the prayer of quiet necessarily presupposes high holiness and great purity of heart. It is precisely because people are not prepared to allow their hearts to be purified that the Lord cannot give this grace.

Can there be exceptions? Of course. But I cannot see that there is any compelling evidence to suggest that, when genuine, 'slaying in the Spirit' is a prayer of quiet. More likely is a quiet state of healing repose. The discernment of the various levels of prayers usually involves a check with the person's general life pattern: the tradition is very strong on this. Teresa looks for growth in humility, fraternal love and detachment. The 'slaying in the Spirit' tends too often to be without a lasting change — say when checked six months later.'[1]

Here, too, as the author points out, we are dealing with two different experiences.

III. The discernment of the great mystics

The great mystics, in particular two noted Doctors of the Church, St Teresa of Avila and St John of the Cross, felt obliged more than once to state their views on mystical experiences from the angle of their bodily effects. Though of different temperaments, both undoubtedly had serious reservations about disciples inclined to overestimate these peripheral phenomena.

---

1. Private letter dated 20 October 1982.

A Controversial Phenomenon

1. St Teresa of Avila

In the *Book of the Foundations,* St Teresa writes of physical weakness and swooning during prayer as follows:

> I may be asked what difference there is between this and rapture, for the two things, at least in appearance, are the same. This is not an unreasonable thing to say, but it is incorrect. The rapture, or union of all the faculties, as I have said, lasts only a short time and leaves in the soul marked effects and an interior light, together with many other benefits: the understanding does not work at all — it is the Lord Who is at work in the will.
>
> In this state the position is very different. The body is captive, but the will, the memory and the understanding are not. Their operations, however, are irregular, and, if by chance they are occupied in a particular subject, they will keep on debating it among themselves all the time.
>
> I find no advantage in this bodily weakness, for it is nothing else. . . . So I advise prioresses to make all possible efforts to prevent these long swoons, for in my opinion they do nothing but paralyse the faculties and senses and hinder them from fulfilling the commands of the soul.[2]

2. St John of the Cross

In *The Ascent of Mount Carmel,* St John of the Cross asks himself what value should be attributed to certain phenomena affecting 'our bodily senses', such as 'seeing figures or persons of the other life', hearing 'extraordinary words', smelling 'fragrant perfumes', savouring a 'delightful taste', and similar sensory impressions received in mystical states.

And what does he say about them?

> It must be known that, although all these things may happen to the bodily senses in the way of God, we must never rely upon them or accept them, but must always fly from them,

---

2. St Teresa of Avila, *Book of the Foundations,* chapter 6.

without trying to ascertain whether they be good or evil; for the more completely exterior and corporeal they are, the less certainly are they of God. For it is more proper and habitual to God to communicate Himself to the spirit, wherein there is more security and profit for the soul, than to sense, wherein there is ordinarily much danger and deception; for bodily sense judges and makes its estimate of spiritual things by thinking that they are as it feels them to be. . . . The bodily sense is ignorant of spiritual things. So he that esteems such things errs greatly and exposes himself to great peril of being deceived; in any case he will have within himself a complete impediment to the attainment of spirituality.[3]

A further remark of St John of the Cross can be usefully applied to the phenomenon that concerns us here:

> If such an experience be of God, it produces its effect upon the spirit at the very moment when it appears or is felt, without giving the soul time or opportunity to deliberate whether it will accept or reject it. For, even as God gives these things supernaturally, without effort on the part of the soul, and independent of its capacity, God produces in it the effect that He desires by means of such things; . . . it is as if fire were applied to a person's naked body; it would matter little whether or not he wished to be burned; the fire would of necessity accomplish its work.

3. A little while ago, Father de Grandmaison, SJ, wrote a few lines that are of value today as an invitation to prudence. Though not presented as a red light, they do at least serve as an amber light or a warning:

> Ecstasy — and here I use the word in the restricted sense of phenomena of inhibition, temporary insensibility,

---

3. St John of the Cross, *The Ascent of Mount Carmel*, Book II, chapter 11.

immobility and contracture, ensuing states of rigidity, partial exemption from the law of gravity, and automatic words and gestures — is not a privilege or a power bestowed on one. It is the price mystics pay for their human fragility. Consequently, it can be reproduced or, more precisely, produced by all kinds of causes. There are natural swoons due to weakness, to highly concentrated thinking, or to excessive efforts to unite with God. There are also demonic, feigned and pathological ecstasies which are the morbid fruits of fraud, hysteria, or even the ingestion of poisons like valerian.[4]

We now have to go further in our analysis. The previous chapters of this second part are by no means a complete answer to the underlying critical questions, but simply show that the major scriptural and mystical references we have examined do not lend themselves to *a priori* claims that the falling phenomenon belongs to a long Christian tradition. Let us now take a closer look at the phenomenon *per se*.

---

4. Quoted by Henri Bremond, *Histoire littéraire du sentiment religieux en France*, vol. II: 'L'invasion mystique', Paris, p. 591.

7

THE AMBIGUITY OF
BODILY MANIFESTATIONS IN GENERAL

The 'falling phenomenon' is an observable fact. But the interpretation of this fact calls for a careful critical analysis. Are we dealing with a phenomenon of the natural order or with an intervention, a special grace, of the Holy Spirit? This, as I said earlier, is the fundamental question.

It is a tricky question to answer, for no one can determine *a priori* and categorically what the Holy Spirit's modes of action will be, or mark out their boundaries.

Moreover, how can one draw a demarcation line between natural, or even pathological, physical manifestations and manifestations that resemble them outwardly but have a spiritual origin?

Yet, if we are unable to determine the Holy Spirit's modes of action positively and *a priori,* we can proceed negatively and rule out those that do not bear his mark. So we can at least establish negative criteria which are a first step towards discernment.

Some of the best insights into the demarcation line itself come from a distinguished expert in this field, Professor Jean Lhermitte, who wrote:

> Many theorists of mystical theology have endeavoured to discover criteria enabling us to distinguish essentially mystical, and therefore preternatural, experiences — like the hearing of voices, visions, ecstasies and raptures — from similar manifestations observed in some subjects who are in no sense mystics.
>
> The truth is that the distinctive features of these two

states, which have very different sources, since the former accord with a supernatural origin while the latter depend exclusively on human nature, become blurred when submitted to rigorous analysis.

The ecstasy of this or that noted invalid in no way differs, in its phenomenology, from the ecstasy experienced by the most authentic mystic. The same is true of the hearing of voices, visions, the fusion of the senses and the sentiment of a presence.

The greatest mystics, like St Teresa of Jesus and St John of the Cross, have warned us against corporeal visions and the hearing of voices, for they were well aware that all these phenomena can be regularly observed in subjects who neither practise asceticism nor experience mystical raptures.

The same holds true of intuitions and insights which are distinguished by an intimate sense of comprehending or apprehending the divine. Of course — and this cannot be too often repeated — any of these phenomena might well, in certain cases, have a divine cause, but their underlying mechanism is merely psycho-physiological.

Some of my patients clearly explain to me that they have such sentiments but cannot believe that they are self-induced. As St Teresa and St John of the Cross tell us, they are 'beings who speak to themselves' unconsciously. The words they hear are but the reflection of their own thoughts.

The same applies to the 'feeling of presence', which is so common in the authentic mystic. Yes, it seems that God is there, present and close to him; of this he is certain. But many of my patients are also haunted by the same feeling of a divine, demonic or human presence, which is but an illusion.

St Teresa was accompanied by an angel armed with a flaming dart. Well, an extremely intelligent and in no sense demented patient of mine believed that, as soon as she stepped out of the house, she was escorted by a resplendent horseman, the image of a cavalry officer who had caught her attention in her youth.

Once again, I wish to make clear that if, from the psycho-physiological or phenomenological viewpoint, I cannot discern in the states I have mentioned any sign entitling me to specify the mystical state, I do not claim that the origin of the said manifestations correspond to one and the same cause. Cannot God be a source of natural inspiration and use psycho-physiological modes which the psychologist is called to understand?

In reality, as the great mystics have professed, starting with St Teresa of Jesus, what confers upon these manifestations the mark of their divine origin is the fruits.

Well, the productions of the pseudo-mystics are trite, whereas the authentic mystics offer us flowers of love and charity.[1]

It is enlightening and useful to know the Church's thinking on the matter of bodily reactions: in former days a decree of the Holy Office prohibited representations of Mary at the foot of the Cross which depicted her swooning or lying unconscious in the arms of St John.

The Church does not wish artists to attenuate or contradict the words of Scripture: 'His mother *stood* by the cross' *(Jn 19:25)*. This attitude of Mary of Calvary was mentioned by the evangelist to emphasise the courage of the one who was more closely associated with the redemptive sacrifice than any other human being. The very image has the value of a symbol and an example.

---

1. *'Les phénomènes mystiques à la lumière de la science contemporaine'*, in *Psychologie contemporaine et christianisme,* pp. 148-49 (a booklet containing articles from *Revue Nouvelle,* Vol. XIX, No. 2, 1953).

8

THE SOVEREIGN FREEDOM AND DISCRETION OF THE HOLY SPIRIT

The preceding remarks bore mainly on human aspects and subjective dispositions regarding God's action. Into those remarks we now have to integrate a criterion of an objective and all-embracing nature which characterises the very action of the Holy Spirit, his sovereign freedom.

The Holy Spirit's action reveals itself by delicate spiritual touches rather than by physical manifestations, spectacular or otherwise. His presence is revealed beyond doubt wherever there is growth in the theological virtues of faith, hope, and love of God and neighbour. Manifestations that are of necessity outward because they are bodily can never prevail over this fundamental criterion.

We also know that the Holy Spirit does not lend himself to any kind of human prediction: he does not allow us to make a rendezvous for him. He does not enter into our pre-established frameworks.

The Holy Spirit works neither in human tumult nor on an assembly line: he does not respect our production lines or our prefabricated sessions. He is the Unpredictable *par excellence* and he cannot be manipulated.

No man can give himself a mystic grace or have it conferred upon him. A mystic grace is not subject to willed repetition and cannot be provoked. The Holy Spirit declines to be fitted into our agendas and timetables, and no human agent can trigger off his action. He eludes our planning and his action does not depend on an atmosphere of collective expectancy.

To get a glimpse of the Spirit's discretion, as a token of his presence, let us reread a page of the *Book of Kings* which reminds us of it so strikingly and poetically:

> Then Yahweh himself went by.
>
> There came a mighty wind, so strong that it tore the mountain and shattered the rocks before Yahweh. But Yahweh was not in the wind.
>
> After the wind came an earthquake. But Yahweh was not in the earthquake.
>
> After the earthquake came a fire, but Yahweh was not in the fire.
>
> After the fire came the sound of a gentle breeze.
>
> When Elijah heard this, he covered his head with his cloak and went out and stood at the entrance of the cave. . . .[1]

This magnificent page of Scripture urges us not to lock God's action into our human categories and to recognise it by the delicacy of its touch.

Everything I have said on the Spirit's unpredictable and sovereignly free action excludes any idea of a healing service conducted with the foreknowledge that the falling phenomenon is bound to occur.

A priori, we may say that 'God's finger is not there'. God's action is not compatible with the many implications of psychological induction, suggestion, etc. We have to respect God's freedom and therefore to stand aloof from anything that, consciously or otherwise, provokes the falling phenomenon in a group, and *a fortiori* in a larger assembly. The more the participants are numerous, the greater is the risk of collective manipulation, mass psychology reactions, and so forth.

In my view, it is most important to exclude any phenomenon of this kind from our liturgical celebrations. At Lourdes priests in vestments were seen falling like ninepins at the close of a ceremony in a chapel.

---

1. *1 Kings 19:11-13.*

Descriptive

One of the priests in question gave me a personal account of the context and the unfolding of this incident.

All this must be carefully avoided.

PART THREE: Pastoral

9

ARE THE 'FRUITS' A DECISIVE CRITERION?

What are we to think, in the present case, of the saying: 'A tree is judged by its fruit'?

Do testimonies witnessing to numerous and excellent fruits suffice to settle this question once and for all and to guarantee the authenticity of the spiritual interpretation?

In chapter 2 we saw that many people who have undergone the experience of 'resting in the Spirit' state that it gave them unexpected feelings of inner peace, joy, letting go to God, spiritual or physical healing, or the sentiment of an extraordinary contact with the Supernatural.

So, should we conclude in favour of the principle that 'a tree is judged by its fruit', and that the salutary effects underlined by these witnesses are in themselves a proof that we are dealing with an extraordinary action of the Spirit?

First, I must point out that we cannot question the subjective testimony and sincerity of the witnesses without objectively connecting the 'effects' to which they attest with the presumed cause, which, in this case, would be an extraordinary intervention of the Spirit.

Logically, we must beware of a conclusion that goes well beyond the premises. We must not jump to the conclusion that because the cause and the fruit are concomitant, there is of necessity a causal relation between them (*cum hoc, ergo propter hoc*), as if the experienced effect were intrinsically bound up with this or that exterior gesture and were a result of it.

Certainly, a tree is judged by its fruit, but we must not be mistaken in identifying the tree, or in evaluating the fruit, or in establishing a link between them.

There are numerous examples of excellent fruits stemming from a cause which is, to say the least, dubious or even completely misinterpreted. I have in mind the short-lived religious awakenings which have occurred here and there throughout the world as a result of some apparition that subsequently proved to be unauthentic. And I am also reminded of Vincent Ferrier's announcement of the end of the world in the fourteenth century, which brought about wonderful fruits of conversion in his listeners.

So we may accept the aforementioned testimonies while reserving judgment on whether or not the causality has been correctly interpreted.

To appreciate the fruits of the falling phenomenon, we must also take a closer look at all of them.

In fact, some may be excellent and others doubtful or bad; some may be immediate but perishable. Some may be recognised instantly, while others need more time to ripen, or are slow to appear, whether good or bad.

There are fruits that can be good and positive at one level, but harmful at other levels: for example, through their repercussions on the group or the collectivity, whose tendency to emotionalism and excitability they might accentuate.

These reflections — and they are by no means exhaustive — have no other aim than to put my readers on their guard against any over-simplification of the problem, applied to the moral field.

In particular, when the phenomenon occurs in the context of an *ad hoc* assembly, the critical mind has to be more than usually alert.

And should anyone regard as 'fruits' certain psychological effects of contentment and inner peace obtained at those moments, I feel bound to point out that various other measures within our human capacity can yield similar results and give rise to better behaviour on the part of the recipients.

Such improvements can also be a specific effect of this or that psychological treatment. So they are not **necessarily** attributable to a particular touch of the Spirit.

Even if prayers and religious gestures 'clothe' and 'envelop' the complex human mechanisms at work, sound spiritual discernment cannot dispense with an analysis of the whole human context.

I have already dealt with the 'tree and fruit' argument in the fourth *Malines Document, Renewal and the Powers of Darkness*,[1] where I applied the same reasoning to do-it-yourself exorcisms whose practitioners have no explicit mandate from the competent authority, but justify their actions by adducing the excellence of the fruits.

I have equally refuted the argument in my book *The Right View of Moral Rearmament*,[2] stating there that we may recognise superior fruits on the moral level yet have serious reservations about them at the doctrinal level.

I quote these examples to widen the horizon and perhaps help my readers to realise that there are numerous areas where the old saying must be carefully interpreted.

1. London, Darton, Longman & Todd, 1983.
2. London, Burns & Oates, 1953.

10

DANGERS INHERENT IN THE EXPERIENCE

I. A preliminary question: should the dangers be pointed out?

The advice sometimes given in healing circles is that no mention should be made of the dangers inherent in the falling and resting phenomenon lest speaking of them proved harmful to God's action.

It is not a good thing, these advisers maintain, to regard 'resting in the Spirit' as a dangerous domain.

The very fact of thinking in terms of danger might foster a mistrustful attitude, which would already be an obstacle to lucid discernment. . .

Such a recommendation prejudges and begs the question. It forbids us, in advance, to examine it and makes 'slaying in the Spirit' one of the graces promised to our time as the fruit of a New Pentecost.

Such a degree of assurance is amazing, but its foundation eludes me.

And how can the same advisers write all this so calmly, without the slightest reference to those to whom the Lord has entrusted the final discernment in his Church?

In contrast with this *a priori* attitude, the following lines, written by a well-known Orthodox theologian, Olivier Clément, urge prudence:

> Faced with this phenomenon as a **collective** experience, we must ask ourselves whether we are dealing with a specifically pneumatic, spiritual experience, or with a psychic one. There is a certain psychic greed which is re-

prehensible. In the Christian East, the attitude is one of very great sobriety and vigilance.[1]

Much the same note of warning is struck by Kevin Perrota, the editor of the American ecumenical review *Pastoral Renewal*, who writes:

> A common difficulty in the Pentecostal charismatic movement is the tendency to confuse spiritual experience with emotional experience. One consequence is that those who are easily aroused emotionally consider themselves to be experiencing life in the Holy Spirit, and being emotional comes to be identified with being spiritual (and vice versa).[2]

We must indeed avoid confusing these two levels and carefully examine the ambiguities and possible dangers underlying the phenomenon.

Both the recipients of this experience and those who make themselves its most prominent advocates are vulnerable to these dangers.

II. Dangers for those playing a passive role

In answer to my request for information, one of my correspondents has of his own accord drawn up the following list of dangers:

1. Some people unconsciously seek not God but to be in the 'in-group' of the latest religious experience, out of curiosity rather than a need for healing, or perhaps because they are looking for the novel and the spectacular.

2. Still unconsciously, some seek attention, because of a psychological or emotional need rather than because they desire to open themselves to a genuine work of the Spirit.

---

1. Quoted in André Fermet, *L'Esprit est notre vie*, Desclée de Brouwer, 1984, p.84.
2. *Pastoral Renewal*, Vol. 8, No. 1, November 1983.

3. Some respond, unconsciously, to a psychological, emotional or hysterical inducement, especially when their leaders have sought to trigger off the 'falling' reaction by a teaching, or by presenting the phenomenon as an integral, normal part of a healing service.

We have to be particularly vigilant when this happens in a disorderly or chaotic way.

4. Some people might also be tempted to measure the work of the Spirit not according to its fruits manifested in ordinary, everyday life, but by the number of those who are 'overcome by the Spirit' at the meeting.

5. Some might be prompted by a feeling of elitist complacency and pride; others again are perplexed because they do not understand what is happening.

This list could be extended much further. My own view, for example, is that some are tempted to seek in the 'falling phenomenon' an answer to their personal problems, which spares them the pain and discipline of solving them by their own efforts, through a more sober life style, self-forgetfulness, forgiveness, etc.

Because, consciously or otherwise, they are eager to find a 'miracle solution', an instant remedy, the falling and resting experience acts as a kind of spiritual anaesthetic.

Father Tardif, who exercises a well-known healing ministry, says that he firmly refuses to respond to the request of those who ask him to pray that they might be 'overcome by the Spirit'. This is a sound pastoral approach.

Another consideration worthy of our attention is the role that the passive person's unconscious desire might play.

If such a person believes that 'resting in the Spirit' is a special grace and aspires to it, he might feel frustrated if he does not obtain it and regard this as a sign that God loves him less than he loves those who fall to the ground.

In this case a number of circumstances combine to trigger off the phenomenon from within, even if he is not fully conscious of the fact and therefore cannot clearly grasp it.

Here I am not speaking of people who suddenly experience the phenomenon without being in the least prepared for it — this is quite another matter — but of those who, in response to an invitation, line up to be overcome by the Spirit and to receive the grace said to reside in falling and resting.

And they do line up: I hear of cases where some queue up several times in succession, impelled by the desire to renew the promised experience.

Some subjects feel frustrated if nothing happens, and almost feel guilty, especially when the intermediary exhorts them with importunate insistence to 'let go to God'.

Lastly, a subtle temptation to self-satisfaction might creep into the experience; and it might easily focus the subject's attention on himself rather than on God's action.

Obviously, this remark is not applicable to everyone, but since human psychology has its own laws, the hypothesis cannot be excluded.

III. Dangers for those playing an active role

Let us now pass on to those who trigger off the phenomenon.

Morton Kelsey, an Anglican pastor and theologian who taught for many years at Notre Dame University, South Bend (USA) and has published a series of psychoanalytical studies, points out a number of dangers which, for the most part, tally with those mentioned above.

The same is true of the writings of Francis MacNutt, although he does not always avoid those dangers in practice. He is not the only one to forget them on the way.

It is disturbing to read, for example, on the jacket of *The Man Behind the Gift*, which relates the life of the author, Father Ralph A. Di Orio (USA), these lines from his text: 'As I walk among you, some of you will feel electricity going through you right out of my body. Heat. A jolt of lightning. Some of you will be falling down.'

Heralded by this kind of announcement and reputation, a religious leader already conditions, by his mere presence, an audience whose expectations are thus aroused. And the 'suggestibility' factor is particularly active in large assemblies.

In my files I have an account of two consecutive healing sessions held in Switzerland. The first is introduced by a Catholic religious in these terms:

Some of you are going to fall down. Don't be afraid. In the Middle Ages there were convents where whole lines of nuns would fall to the ground. They were touched by God, like Paul on the road to Damascus and the soldiers at Gethsemane. The Lord will take care of you, too, so that when you fall, you won't hurt yourselves. . .

Then the account of the first session continues in this vein:

Madame X got up to speak and referred to personal dialogues with God, visions and successful healings. To conclude, she said: 'Now, at this very moment, some of you are aleady healed. The Lord is touching you now: at this moment a cancer is healed; and also coronary arteries; and also a cancer which must not be operated, for the Spirit does the operating. At this moment kidney stones are being dissolved through the blood of Christ'.

And here is the account of the second session:

This session began with the witness of those who were healed at the previous session. They testified to their experiences.
 The session lasted for over two hours; hymns and repeated refrains were punctuated by healing stories from the Bible and by advice about the best position to take in order to fall painlessly.
 The air was becoming more and more close. At times the healers worked with the aid of special effects.[3]

Undoubtedly, the dangers are obvious in the case of a large-scale assembly of the Kathryn Kuhlman variety. They are

---

3. Further details and critical remarks are provided by a Swiss writer who has made a special study, as an observer, of the conditioning of large assemblies: Karl Guido Rey, *Gotteserlebnisse im Schnellverfahren. Suggestion als Gefahr und Charisma*, Ed. Kösel, 1985.

A Controversial Phenomenon

reduced when the phenomenon assumes a more discreet and gentle form.

But, even then, I feel that it is an exaggeration to claim that it is 'a kind of mystical experience, at least as far as the fruits are concerned'.

11

IS IT A NATURAL PHENOMENON OR A SIGN OF THE HOLY SPIRIT'S ACTION?

I. Is the phenomenon natural or not?

Pursuing our study of the phenomenon as such, we still have to ask ourselves a final question which goes well beyond the by-no-means hypothetical dangers I have pointed out: are we dealing with a natural phenomenon, or with a special intervention of the Spirit which transcends the forces of nature?

Thus we are touching upon the always delicate relations between nature and grace: where does nature end and grace begin?

On the one hand, the action of grace, operating directly on the human being, is a subtle concept to define, for it intimately espouses the contours of the human factors; it does not run beside them like a parallel line.

On the other, the term 'nature' is equally complex: Lalande's *Philosophical Dictionary* provides eighteen different definitions of it. Moreover, any definition we may adopt is necessarily static. It cannot demarcate the area of the unknown natural forces: some of them are not yet understood by the human mind, and it is only with the help of tomorrow's new scientific discoveries that we will be able to master them. The list of scientific discoveries which have gradually extended man's powers is unending.

Let us bear in mind these words of St Augustine: 'The mysteries of the Invisible do not contradict nature; they merely contradict what **we** know of nature.'

The nature-grace relationship has been expressed with rare accuracy, in regard to the Holy Spirit's role, by Father Adrien

Demoustier, SJ, in his article entitled *The Holy Spirit's Intervention*, which deals with the Charismatic Movements:

> The sanctifying Spirit and the creative Spirit are one and the same. Consequently, the Holy Spirit's sanctifying action not only respects and uses the elements of our human existence, but also increases their value and strengthens them. The Holy Spirit therefore sanctifies and manifests his sanctifying work by acting on those aspects of our life which at another level, and quite rightly, are analysed by psychology, sociology, and so on. And this action of the Holy Spirit, so far from invalidating these analyses or rendering them superfluous, requires us, on the contrary, to make a more serious and truthful use of them.
>
> By sanctifying man, the Spirit respects and accentuates the autonomy of the human experience. All the manifestations of his action are manifestations in man's spirit. This spirit of man always remains distinct from the Spirit of God. At the very moment when they have to be interpreted as authentic signs of his personal intervention, the manifestations of the Holy Spirit remain human actions that have to be understood and directed according to the rules of human knowledge and wisdom.
>
> The laws of psychological, sociological, economic and political behaviour remain fully valid, and even acquire a greater urgency through the intensity of the spiritual experience, because the Spirit of God intervenes to make his action known to us.
>
> Because they are prompted by the Holy Spirit, charismatic phenomena in the strict sense of the word — glossolalia, prophecy, healing, etc. — are human phenomena fairly well understood by specialists in mankind's religious experience. They regularly occur when a certain number of circumstances are combined. It is together with this acquired knowledge of their causes and consequences that they are signs of the Holy Spirit's action.[1]

1. *Christus* 93, Tome 24, January 1977.

Pastoral

II. Unknown forces of nature

The Holy Spirit espouses human action, penetrates it and leads it to goals that lie beyond us. But we should not too hastily attribute to him a direct intervention transcending or excluding the interplay of natural forces.

The field of natural forces is immense, but the field of natural forces that are still unexplored or under investigation stretches before us and is becoming vaster every day. The history of science demonstrates this abundantly: with each new discovery, natural forces gradually yielding their secrets and their laws are brought to light.

These discoveries in no way restrict God's creative power, which remains the prime cause of the cosmos, while ceasing to be, as it was for our ancestors, the direct and exclusive cause of particular phenomena, such as storms or rainbows. New discoveries do not lessen God's sovereign power over the universe, but only our ignorance.

What is true of every sphere of nature is particularly true of the exploration of man's powers.

Extraordinary psychic phenomena have always existed. For many centuries they were considered supernatural, or sometimes even diabolical; only gradually did they come to be seen as natural.

It was from the time of the German doctor Mesmer (1734-1815) and his followers that men came to recognise the existence of physiological radioactivity: mesmerism has helped to develop increasingly the psychomagnetic energies latent in each human being.

Present-day science tells us that the human brain has so far put into action only a tiny fraction of its real potential.

It is from modern science that we have learned something about hypnotism, suggestion, telekinesis, therapeutic or experimental magnetic wave motion, the visibility of human auras or emanations, and cataleptic, comatose or somnambulistic states.

For our present purpose, it is useful to consult researches into partial hypnosis which show that falling backwards (or forward) is an integral part of group therapies and of taught exercises. Important factors here are the partial immobilisation of the subject through suggested inhibition or other experiences of induced automatism.

Equally relevant to our subject are current researches into psychological or parapsychological phenomena. I mention these not because they provide a firm answer, but to show the complexity of interpreting the 'falling phenomenon'.

1. In psychology, it is advisable to examine everything observable in this phenomenon which might be explained by suggestion, auto-suggestion, hypnotism, mass psychology, the working of the unconscious and psychosomatic experiences.

When the phenomenon is produced by touch, it would also be of interest to question specialists in a recently created branch of therapy which might shed some light on the problem: known as 'touch therapy', it has received some publicity and is taking its place among the latest medical practices.

An American journal *Woman's Day* (26 June 1979) published an article on the subject which tells us that a new category of healers are helping to relieve illness by laying-on of hands. It underlines that the scientific world cannot explain the **how** of the remedy but notes that it works.

The founder of this branch of medicine, Dolores Kriegen, who lectures at the University of New York, has published certain findings of her research under the title *Therapeutic Touch: How to Use Your Hands to Help or to Heal.*

A field also worth exploring, as an element that might, in some cases, be operative is **hypnosis** or self-hypnosis. Father G. Maloney, SJ, writes:

> Although I have never been 'slain', mainly because I never wanted to let go in this manner, I have been hypnotised and I have hypnotised many people. In hypnosis one can acquire a tremendous feeling of peace, of moving almost out of the body, of floating toward Heaven. A religious person can direct this toward God, but getting there is a simple, natural method, a technique. We must not turn away from techniques in prayer. But we must realise that techniques are not prayer.

The same theologian wrote to Morton Kelsey that he had himself studied these phenomena under the direction of a non-Christian parapsychologist who was able to provoke them without any reference to God.

This fact deserves special attention, for the absence of any religious reference in the case of that practitioner obliges us to examine the phenomenon *per se* with extra care, and without too hastily giving our analysis a religious interpretation. It urges us to be prudent in our interpretation.

I should add — always at the psychological level — that an adequate evaluation of the phenomenon must take account of what occurs in the practice of natural methods of relaxation which produce certain similar partial effects.

2. Moving on from psychology to other fields of inquiry that are still only partly explored, we note that researches in these fields are becoming increasingly wide-ranging and giving rise to wholly new problems.

Investigators tell us of electromagnetic fields radiating from all living beings and forming a kind of 'aura' that can be photographed, measured, etc.

Each day our discoveries are enriched by new findings concerning paranormal phenomena, and the as yet unexplored potential of man and his brain. The development of researches in these domains would be of great value, for all these new discoveries illustrate the words of St Irenaeus: 'God's glory is living man.'

In his study *Supernature: a Natural History of the Supernatural* (London, Hodder and Stoughton, 1973), the biologist Lyall Watson has devoted a whole chapter to the mind's hidden powers over matter.

And very probably tomorrow will bring us more and more advanced scientific studies on phenomena like telepathy or the transmission of thoughts and mental images.

According to Charles Honorton, Director of the Parapsychology Department of the Moses Maimonides Hospital in New York, new discoveries are on the horizon. He writes in a letter that if, as his experiments lead him to believe, telepathic communication becomes a common human faculty, this would imply the existence of an as yet unknown factor inherent in a higher form of matter; the discovery of this factor or form of energy would be as important as the discovery of nuclear energy.

Although I am not competent to judge this matter, I am convinced that we must remain open to what might be revealed, tomorrow, as a new dimension in our knowledge of man.

I conclude with another directly received testimony.

A priest who had practised 'resting in the Spirit' for some years, then gave it up, primarily through obedience to his bishop, and subsequently through personal conviction, described to me as 'an electric current' the rather painful burning sensation he used to feel in his hands when he stretched them over sick and healthy people alike.

He wholly ceased to practise this 'induced resting', but he told me that, even now, when he lectures from a rostrum and makes an eloquent gesture with his hands, people in the first row of the audience sometimes fall backwards.

How do we account for this type of influx?

I am as much in the dark about it as he is, but I have no reason to doubt the truth of his statement.

My sole conclusion, at the experimental level, is that we are only just beginning to understand certain phenomena and that many new discoveries await us.

12

ON THE NECESSITY OF CAUTION

We cannot close our eyes to the falling phenomenon or fail to see that it has become widespread throughout the Church's Charismatic Renewal and therefore leaves many question marks.

We have to take a pastoral position on this issue, and directives must be given by the competent authorities.

While the survey mentioned in chapter 2 was being conducted, I questioned quite a few theologians and psychologists from various countries.

Generally speaking, they were united in the view that the falling phenomenon must be approached with caution.

I. Here, to begin with, is an answer provided by a Theological and Pastoral Study Group, questioned on the subject by the National Service Committee of the Charismatic Renewal for the Catholic Church in Ireland. Its main statements are as follows:

> Pastorally, we suggest:
>
> a) that the term 'slaying in the Spirit' should at all times be avoided as this inclines people immediately to the discernment that it is, or may very likely be, from God. We think it is far better to follow the Rev. John Richards in adopting the neutral term 'falling'. That accurately describes what happens and leads to a more objective and unprejudiced discernment as to **why** they have fallen.
>
> b) We would always discourage circumstances in which the phenomenon would occur.
>
> c) We would not invite ministers whose prayer or teaching is associated with this phenomenon.
>
> d) In speaking about 'slaying in the Spirit', we would

always adopt a negative approach, leaving open the possibility, however, that on some very few occasions this may be a gift from God.

We would not encourage people in any way to look for a genuine 'falling' as a grace, since this will leave them open to self-induced 'fallings'. . . .

II. The German theologian, Professor Heribert Mühlen, who has written some authoritative works on the Holy Spirit, points out at the end of a study that I had requested from him privately:

Falling backwards, letting go physically, can be **a psychological aid** leading to a deeper self-surrender to God.

In accordance with the principle of the discernment of spirits, I believe that the phenomenon *per se* is of a psychological and therapeutic nature, and is out of place in a religious service.

Only qualified psychiatrists and doctors should concern themselves with it, for reactions of a medical nature may need care and attention.

III. And here is a reply from Father Yves Congar, OP, who, as we know, has just completed several important volumes on the Holy Spirit.

Having interviewed a few people acquainted with the facts, he sent me his reflections on 'resting in the Spirit':

Once we have taken note of the external physical facts, and even the internal psychological facts, we are not entitled necessarily to attribute to the Holy Spirit effects that may be brought about by psychic forces which the 'charismatic' practice may have liberated or awakened.

We must be wary of induced reactions. Has there been a free response to a secret and personal visit from God? An aspect of quietism is also to be feared.

Of course, God invites us to surrender ourselves to him (cf. Thérèse of Lisieux), but our self-surrender should keep us on our feet and make us active (cf. *Ez 1:1-2*).

Those who undergo this experience describe their feeling as one of self-abandonment, **a loss of egocentric consciousness,** a sensation of peace, warmth and weightlessness. Here we find the danger that so obviously threatened the Corinthians in St Paul's time. They indulged in their experiences of *pneumatika*. . . . They tended to be less interested in the Holy Spirit, in God, than in his gifts; the danger of spiritual greed, denounced by the mystics, is not a fantasy.[1]

Also from France, I have received the carefully qualified and considered conclusion of a survey, which I would like to quote.

The eighth Annual Meeting of Jesuits of the Charismatic Renewal, held near Paris in January 1983, studied the topic 'resting in the Spirit' and subsequently published its findings under the title *Resting in the Spirit: Principles of Discernment*.

The Assembly's general conclusion about this complex phenomenon ends as follows:

> Bearing in mind the very real danger of deviation, the very prudent attitude of the Church's pastors, and lastly the fact that the charismatic life is not dependent on 'resting in the Spirit', we are of the opinion that it would be better not to introduce or encourage this phenomenon in the Catholic Charismatic Renewal.

I too am reaching the same conclusion.

IV. A charism for our time?

Pursuing the same line of thought, I wish to say, first of all, that it is inappropriate to write that if one questions this particular 'charism', one is calling all the other charisms into question, as a publicity leaflet states.

Or again, to maintain that the falling phenomenon is identical to the phenomenon of glossolalia.

---

1. *Private letter* dated 5 April 1982.

Those who hold this view are disregarding the biblical foundation of glossolalia, which, moreover, should not be interpreted as a miraculous gift of speaking in unknown tongues.

At all events, it is wrong to associate the fate of the 'falling phenomenon' with that of the charisms recognised and vouched for by the Church's tradition.

Besides, there are charisms and charisms: their variety is such that they do not have a uniform meaning.

St Paul lists a number of ordinary charisms which give natural gifts a supernatural goal, and his list is by no means exhaustive.

The gifts of the Spirit range from administration, teaching, preaching, catechesis to the care of the sick. And, of course, this list could be extended much further.

V. Do not prejudge

A phenomenon must be presumed to be natural until the contrary can be proved. The obligation to demonstrate the contrary falls on the person who claims that it is supernatural.

Such a prudent approach is not a lack of faith, or a sign of unconscious rationalism, but simply a practical application of the Church's traditional teaching on the relation between nature and grace.

To avoid muddled thinking on this subject, it would be advisable to give the circles where the phenomenon occurs a teaching on the relations between nature and grace, and particularly on the intervention in human behaviour of somatic, psychic and spiritual factors.

In this way infectious excitability could be avoided.

From the more general viewpoint which I am adopting here, my task is not to determine the nature of the phenomenon or the interpretation to be attributed to it in specific, individual cases.

I can only take note of authentic testimonies, and I remain indebted to my correspondents for their generous response to my appeal. It is not for me to make categorical judgments about particular personal experiences.

But it is appropriate to issue general pastoral guidelines in regard to the context in which this phenomenon and its variants occur: prayer groups, larger gatherings, eucharistic celebrations; and also in regard to the 'specialists' of various countries who claim to have this gift.

VI. Seek the Church's advice

To fail to seek the advice of one's bishop as to whether or not this phenomenon is in line with the Church's tradition is not a normal procedure.

Nor is it normal, as I have pointed out more than once, to keep one's bishop uninformed about the occurrence of this phenomenon, lest he should be opposed to its widespread practice and expresses doubts as to its wisdom.

There is no place in God's holy Church for a religious practice which remains on the fringe of the common Christian life and is reserved for a privileged few.

It is important, I believe, for the spiritual health of Christians that they should understand clearly that the whole Church is charismatic by its very nature. Consequently, there is no such thing as two Churches: the 'institutional' Church on the one hand, and the 'charismatic' Church on the other.

The very term 'institutional' sets the Church's hierarchy within a sociological framework, and we all know the extent to which 'institutions' are the object of criticism and rejection.

The Church is a 'sacramental' reality, and this term gets down to the root of the matter. It means that bishops-priests-deacons have been invested by the Holy Spirit at their ordination or consecration, and have received a permanent charism at the service of the people of God.

Those charisms remain and form part of the very structure of the visible Church. The charisms which concern all the baptised are gifts bestowed by the Spirit — manifestations of his presence — with a view to upbuilding the Church. But they are gifts bestowed at baptism, for that particular purpose, which means that they are not inherent in the person who claims that they are his. A man is never the permanent recipient of this or that gift; still less does he own it.

This point must be underlined if we wish to accept the mystery of the Church in the fullest sense and live by it: the

Church is built on the foundation of the Apostles — and of their successors, the bishops; and in the final reckoning, the duty and responsibility of judging the prophets and interpreting the charisms devolves on them.

So it is important that, with full knowledge of the facts and in an atmosphere of mutual openness, they should be able to exercise their pastoral function and guide the people of God.

A highway code is not designed to obstruct traffic: it is a safeguard enabling motorists to advance safely on the road and to avoid accidents.

It is in this perspective of faith that we have to set the problems facing us, in order to ensure the flowering of God's gifts among us, and primarily to guarantee their authenticity.

CONCLUSION

We thus return to the real issue of the debate: 'resting in the Spirit' is a controversial phenomenon but, more importantly, it threatens the authenticity and credibility of the 'Pentecostal' Charismatic Renewal.

Here we see how greatly the visible and the invisible Church need to live in a state of integration. The bishops, as the spiritual guides of the People of God, have to be close to the faithful, particularly in these delicate matters, in order to avoid deviations and a loss of vital energy. It is also their duty to invite the Church's best theologians to offer and share with Christians of good will the treasures of wisdom of our mystics and of the great spiritual tradition of Western and Eastern Christendom.

The gifts of the Spirit, like the moral virtues, must be lived not in the abstract, but in the concrete mobility of particular situations. In this respect we are called to a renewal which, springing from the source, the Holy Spirit, adapts itself to the nature of the soil and the diversity of the terrain.

Our spiritual and moral teaching has all too often been poured into rigid moulds, and it must also be renewed in the Spirit.

Faced with new phenomena which affect the spiritual life, we have to give the faithful guidelines: red, green or amber lights. This is the very precondition of true and sure progress.

A policy of non-intervention falls short of what the faithful are entitled to expect of their spiritual guides. But warnings are not enough: they must be perceived as appeals to genuine fidelity amid the variety of the Spirit's gifts and charisms.

This sixth *Malines Document* aims to clear a path in order to contribute, subsequently, towards the renewal of everything in the ministry and pastoral work of healing, both being an integral part of the redemptive Incarnation.

Christ the Saviour of man is also he who heals man's wounds. His Church has the duty to continue his ministry of healing, to pursue the combat against the Powers of Evil, and to recognise, authenticate and encourage the development of the charism of healing by charting safe roads for it.[1]

Besides, I believe that a problem like the one we have just examined equally urges us to pursue our search for an ever-increasing harmony between nature and grace. Their interpenetration is essential since it prevents the full blossoming of nature from degenerating into naturalism and our response to the supernatural from deviating into supernaturalism.[2]

Throughout the history of the Church we observe this same problem of perfect balance arising each time one of two complementary aspects is overvalued to the detriment of the other.

I have always been fond of this thought expressed by a character in one of Claudel's plays: 'I love contradictory things that exist simultaneously. Grace and nature have to blossom simultaneously, in response to God's thought about man, whom he wishes to be a responsible being, standing on his feet, while at the same time offering himself to man with total gratuitousness, in order to enrich him with his wonderful gifts which surpass all our human hopes.'[1]

---

1. L.-J. Suenens, *Renewal and the Powers of Darkness,* London, Darton, Longman and Todd, 1982.
2. L.-J. Suenens, *Nature and Grace, a Vital Unity,* chapter I, London, Darton, Longman and Todd, 1985.